FULLBACK

A True-Life Story of Resilience and Determination

Larry "Tank" Perdue

DEDICATION

This book is dedicated to my mother, Lucille Perdue. You encouraged and influenced me in so many ways. My character and resilience are the manifestations of your love and guidance. My only regret is that I couldn't reward you for everything that you've done for me, mama. I miss you dearly, and I always think about how much your granddaughters would have enjoyed your presence. Thank you for molding me into the man I am today. May you rest in Heaven and continue to be of service to God. I dedicate this book to my big sister, Charlotte Perdue. At times the "tough love" was a little too tough, but one thing that was always for certain, the "love" was there. I thank you for your protection and support. I miss you terribly and love you dearly, sis. May you rest in heaven peacefully. I dedicate this book to ALL of my old teammates and coaches from both Milwaukee Marshall and Pasadena Marshall Fundamental high schools, respectively. Through the sport of football, we have forged great friendships, and continue to interact with each other to this day.

I would also like to give a shout out to all of the great FULLBACKS that have inspired me with their tenacious and selfless efforts on the football field. Great players like Jim Brown, Marion Motley, Larry Csonka, Mike Alstott and Craig"Ironhead" Hayward. I also admired men like Earl Campbell, Jerome Bettis, Brandon Jacobs, Christian Okoye and many others that ran the rock with violent intentions and unwavering determination. This book is dedicated to all of the guys that had the testicular fortitude to play one of the most demanding positions in football. **FULLBACK.**

PREFACE

"Hey man, do you play football?" "You look like a football player." "So, where did you play ball, big man?" "You are a little stocky, thick dude, were you a fullback?" "Man, I know you played football." "Little man is gonna be a football player." I have heard these statements and declarations almost all of my life. So much, that sometimes I can't help but to think if I had missed my true calling in life. The sport of football has been like that one love that will always have a special place in your heart. No matter how many times she may have broken your heart in the past, whenever she wants you, you go back to her. Football is my love jones. I love the sport and I hate the sport. But I credit the sport with providing me the qualities and character that I needed to become a man. I now have a renewed love for the sport of football.

Why did I title this book, "FULLBACK?" Well, I truly admired the physicality and toughness that the position required. And sometimes you may have to approach your personal struggles, tribulations and adversities like a big, strong, fast Fullback. Sometimes you may have to display a certain type of grit and strong will to endure and get the job done. What was once a very important position in football, is now just a little more than a temporary extension of the offensive line. Fullbacks went from carrying the load of the offense, to total irrelevance in the modern era of football. The passing game in football has evolved. The game is now played at a faster pace, and is considered to be more exciting than in the past. Nowadays some teams don't even have a fullback on their roster. (That's a damn shame!) Other than goal-line packages and "cosmetic" looks to give a defense, the fullback is a scarcely implemented position. The fullback has now officially been added to the extinction list. Save the fullback position, football coaches!!!

Table of Contents

Larry "Tank" Perdue

"You Ain't No Basketball Player, Fatboy!"

Life can be like a gang-tackling bunch of wild, blood thirsty linebackers. Merciless and relentless. And you find yourself colliding with these linebackers, play after play. You keep getting up off the ground, ignoring the pain. But the glory comes with every hard yard that you rush the ball for, or every block that protects your quarterback or springs your halfback for a huge gain or a touchdown. Life is like smash mouth football. At times it may hit extremely hard, but you just gotta absorb the blows, man up and hit back, twice as hard.

I was born in Milwaukee, Wisconsin, at St. Luke's hospital on the afternoon of March 30th, 1971. I am the product of a single-parent, low-income home which consists of my mother Lucille (may God bless her sweet soul), my big brother Ralph, my big sister Charlotte (R.I.H) and I, Boobie. My father, LC, was a married man that lived on the other side of town with his wife and kids. Growing up, I was always a highly energetic kid. Sometimes my hyper-activity would get me into all kinds of trouble. My mother told me stories of how I would get scratched up and bitten by our pet cats and dogs. I would do cruel things like trying to flush the pets down the toilet or trying to ride them, "like a horsey." Or the time that I busted into a room full of company donning my "Superman" outfit (tight, white briefs and a bath towel tied around my neck) and yelled, "Superman!" Then I climbed on top of the couch, jumped over the coffee table and ended up knocking myself out cold. As most young boys, I displayed some pretty destructive and anxious behavior growing up. But once I was introduced to sports, I began to learn that there's a place for my aggressive behavior. My introduction to sports wasn't through an organized youth league or tossing the ball around in the yard with Dad. Growing up on the north side of Milwaukee, we played a lot of sports in the streets. We played Baseball, Football, Basketball and Kickball on our neighborhood streets, as well as other little games that actually helped develop skills. Games like, "cans", "king of the hill" and "home run derby" actually challenges kids to express their individual athleticism in competitive settings. I think that you initially realize your competitive nature and signs of athletic ability when you're a child, playing with other children. I noticed that I was often shorter and heavier than other kids my age, but I also realized that I could run just as fast, jump just as high as every other kid I played with.

My truest introduction to football was not through playing in the street, or on a field at school or the park, but in a shoebox. I had a friend that enjoyed collecting comic books, I enjoyed collecting comics as well. We often would swap copies or borrow them from each other. One day, I bought a few packs of comic books, went home and realized that I already had a few of the issues. So I took the comic books over to Marty's house, hoping to make a swap. I browsed through Marty's comic book collection, but couldn't find anything that I didn't already have. So then Marty pulls out a shoebox. "What's that?" I ask. "Cards." "Football cards",

Marty says. "You like football, don't you?" "You be playin' with us all the time. Check these out." Hmmm. Football cards. I only played street football. I never really followed the game, and I never was a fan of the star players. But something about these cards had me mesmerized. The bright colors of the uniforms, the athletic moves and positions by the players that were caught in the photos on the cards amazed me. The big, nappy afros, the funny looking mustaches and beards that symbolized the "70's, were creatively attractive to me. Before these football cards, I would try to watch football games on TV with my brother, but I would wander off after five minutes or so, because it would eventually bore me. You couldn't see the players faces to make an identifiable connection, like basketball and baseball. But the cards gave football players a personality. A face to match with the number. On the back of the cards were the players bios and stats. Man, these football cards are cool, I thought. So I swapped comic books for all of Marty's duplicate football cards. This transaction would also lead to my stint as a sports card collector. I began to buy and trade football, basketball and baseball cards with other kid collectors. I think I gave up collecting sports cards and comic books when I hit puberty. I began to grow more of an interest in girls than those childish sports cards and comic books. (Wish I had those collections now, dummy!)

Now you would think that the "shoebox" was the catalyst to my love affair with football, and I'm sure that this will be surprising to some, but basketball, actually, was my first love. No one could tell me that I wasn't going to be an NBA star. "You're too short and too big to be a basketball player!", people would say. Kids would laugh at me and argue over who would guard the little fat dude. But what people didn't see was the drive and determination that was fed by every negative comment about my size and stature.

During my elementary years, I tried to play basketball every day. You couldn't catch me without a basketball in my hands. I would steal basketballs from school and bring them home, to make sure that I always had a basketball. I was a basketball fanatic. I was crazy in love with the sport. In the 6th grade, I was good enough to be selected to play in my school's All-Star game, which concluded our intramural league season. The top 2 players from each team were selected. My sisters' boyfriend drove me to the game that fateful night. I didn't have the "all-star" performance that I wanted to have. My stat line was 2-4, 4 points, 4 assists and a steal. And my team lost the game, as well. I was crushed. I just knew that I was a much better player than what I had shown that night. After the game and on the way home, Darryl, my sisters' boyfriend laid it to me straight. He didn't spare my feelings and was totally honest with me. He said "Boobie, this ain't your sport." I responded with, "everybody says that, but they also say that I can ball!"

"I made it to the all-star game, man I know I can play." Darryl said "yeah, you can play, but hoop ain't your sport, man. Football is your sport. You're a running back. A fullback! You should be playing football." "You know what people were saying every time you touched the ball tonight?" Darryl continued. They said things like, "look at the little fat boy!" "That little fat boy can dribble! "Little dude is so fast although he's chunky." "They weren't talking about how tall you were, or how great of a player you were", Daryl stated matter-of-factly. I was stunned. People thought that I was just a short, fat kid that appeared to be very athletic, despite what they thought were physical limitations. It hurts to be judged by your appearance, than by your skill level, " I know what your sport is", Daryl quipped. "Football". "You could be like a Earl Campbell, Larry Csonka-type dude. "A big running back!" I've heard of those names before. I had their football cards. Daryl's blunt assessment and opinions hurt me to the core. But it was a sobering reality. I may not have a future in basketball, after all.

FULLBACK

Larry "Tank" Perdue

"A Harsh Reality and a Dying Dream"

On June 26, 1983, my mother and I moved to California in search of a better life. Why California? My mother had been dating this guy, Robert, who was from California. Robert was temporarily living in Milwaukee with his sister. Why? I don't know why. All I knew is that my mother had been dating this guy for a few months, and suddenly we're getting ready to move to California. I tried to be optimistic about the move, but deep down I was saddened and heartbroken. I knew that I was going to miss my friends and family. The only place I could remember ever traveling to was Chicago, which was an annual trip. California? We didn't have family out there and we didn't know anybody out there. And we never had been there for a visit. As most kids do, I would try to fight my depression with unrealistic dreams and expectations. "The Lakers play in California!" I thought to myself. "I'm gonna meet Magic Johnson!" "I'm gonna play basketball at a great school and have a great life!" Sometimes your dreams are the only barrier between anxiety and depression. Unfortunately, our struggles in Milwaukee and California were the same. We arrived in LA homeless. My mothers' boyfriend, Robert, had left for California about a few weeks before us. Robert was supposed to have secured a job and a home before we arrived. Robert hadn't accomplished either goal. He was living with another sister (Robert had 5 sisters) in LA and didn't tell her that his girlfriend and her 12-year-old son from Milwaukee were coming to live. Fortunately, Robert's sister took us in, but made him move down the street to live with yet another of his 4 sisters. (Yes, Robert had three sisters that had homes on the same neighborhood block). I also learned quickly that the "hood" is the "hood", no matter where you're at. I found California to be very intriguing. How could a place so beautiful be so dangerous? How can anybody be mad out here? If I remember correctly, we lived with Robert's sister on 92nd and Hoover, which was Hoover crip territory. Milwaukee had gangs but this shit was ridiculous! The gangs in LA were very active. And they seemed to be everywhere. Our first night in LA, I couldn't sleep because the sound of random gun fire had me shook! Even when I visited Chicago, I never heard so much gun fire. The next day, I was sent to the liquor store to buy some snacks. My mother had bought me a brand new "Magic Johnson" basketball and a red and white converse short set, right before we left Milwaukee. The gifts were actually offerings to ease my grief. So I decided to wear the red and white converse shirt and shorts on my first day as a Californian. As I walked down the block dribbling my basketball and taking in my new environment, a group of kids ran up on me, smiling and laughing. They were yelling at me, "what's up cuz!" "What set you from fool!" I had no idea what they were talking about, and they were some very scary looking dudes, too. I tried to explain that I had just moved from Milwaukee, but they really weren't trying to hear it. They jumped me. I felt blows coming from every direction. These dudes were beating me as if I had spit on their grandmama's! All I could do was curl up on the ground and protect my face. I kept yelling, "I ain't from here!" "I'm not a cuz!" I repeated. Then I heard a voice say, "cuz leave this little nigga alone." It was one of the OGs of the hood. An "OG" is usually a gang member that's an older adult, and has some influence over the "BG's", which are the younger gang members. The group stopped beating me, but for some sadistic reason, tried to drag me and throw me on top of a dead dog that was left on the sidewalk after being struck by a car! I fought back ferociously! I was not going to let these guys drop me on top of a dead dog! I'd rather take the beating. The OG insisted ("get off of him before I slap the shit outta y'all") and the group of young thugs walked away, laughing. The OG walked away too, without saying one word to me. I ran back to Roberts' sister's apartment to tell everyone what happened to me. I was so scared and shook that I didn't want to leave the apartment. But Robert's sister explained to me that kids are going to "charge me up" about my gang affiliation everywhere I go." I'll never be in a gang." I thought. Then she sent me back to the store to buy some snacks.

I eventually became friends with the same group of kids that jumped me. And I still had to "squab" (squabble, fight) with the "homies" (friends) to prove

that I had "heart". (Fearless, not afraid) The street slang

was much different in California. Some guys were safer

to hang out with than others. Some of the guys enjoyed

playing sports like I did. We would go to the local school

to play basketball and eat lunch every day. That summer

recreation program helped to keep me out of the grip of

the streets. The first time I saw a drive-by shooting, I just

couldn't believe how bold those guys were. And I

couldn't understand why these guys out here were so

willing to commit murder or die over gang colors. Crack

cocaine and sherm were the drugs of choice, and I saw

how people were sucked into the funnel of addiction. I

saw kids younger than me with guns under their waist

bands, pulling bank rolls out of their pockets at the

corner store, riding brand new mopeds and driving nice

cars. I also saw kids reppin' their sets, with no fear,

anxious to get into some gangsta shit. For me, it was a

long, hard summer in LA. As I mentioned before, my

mothers' boyfriend, Robert, had a total of 5 sisters. We

ended up living with 4 of his sisters by the end of the summer.

My mothers' relationship with Robert quickly went sour. She realized that Robert was an alcoholic and a crackhead. Robert also began to physically abuse my mother and that's when she began the process of trying to leave that asshole. Roberts' sister, Linda, was sympathetic to my mothers' situation. She allowed us to live with her and her family while my mother searched for a job and tried to establish residency, so we could apply for emergency benefits. Due to issues in their past, Robert was not on good terms with Linda and was not allowed to come to her house. For some reason, Robert feared his sister Linda, and he stopped harassing my mother. The summer was winding down, and it was time to find a junior high school to enroll at. My mother had begun to date a guy named Don, who was also Linda's cousin. Don lived in Altadena, California. He would drive to LA mostly on weekends to see Linda and other family members. As mom and Don courted, the relationship between my mother and Linda began to deteriorate.

Larry "Tank" Perdue

After spending a few days with Don in Altadena, my mother accepted Don's offer to move in with him. So again, we're on the move, and the summer isn't even over yet.

Life in Altadena was a little slower than the pace in LA. A small town with beautiful landmarks, Altadena was the change of scenery my mother and I desperately needed. I began my 7th grade year at Wilson junior high school, in Pasadena. I immediately participated in youth basketball leagues at the local boys and girls club and at church. But I was still having trouble transitioning to attending school in California. I had no family members or friends at the school, and I often clashed with bullies and mean girls. Due to behavior issues and unsatisfactory academic performance, my mother and I agreed that I needed to attend another school. So I transferred to Marshall fundamental school. It is now my 8th grade year, and I am attending Marshall fundamental. The school has a big, beautiful campus and I also have a few friends from the neighborhood to associate with. When basketball season rolled around, I tried out for the 8th grade basketball team. I made the final cut and earned the starting point guard position. Yes, the same short, fat kid from Milwaukee that was told that i'm too fat to be a basketball player. I still displayed the athletic ability and competitive will that I played with in grade school. I didn't have great stats, but I could still handle the rock and pass it on a string. I am also proud to say that during those rather youthful years, I was blessed to play with guys like ex-NBA star Tracy Murray and Jon Jon Herald, ex-member of the R&B group TROOP. I won a boys club championship with Tracy and a church league championship with Jon Jon, respectively. Those were great times for me. But my break-up with basketball would be ugly.

During my freshman year in high school, at Marshall fundamental, I attempted to make the freshman basketball team. But I had missed two days of a three-day try-out. I attended the third day of try-outs and didn't perform at a high level. Needless to say, I didn't make the team. At first, I blamed everybody and everything but myself. If I hadn't been skipping classes so much, especially gym class, I would've found out about the try-outs on time. I would've been ready to play. But I couldn't ignore the things that I realized about this particular basketball try-out. The kids were bigger and more skilled. The pace of play was much faster and intense, as I could sense the desperation from these kids trying to make the team. Realizing that my hoop dreams were over, I began to rekindle my interest into that other sport...

FULLBACK

"Boy Meets Football"

It is now the summer before my sophomore year (1986) at Marshall fundamental, and some of my friends are getting ready for summer football camp. Although my friends were very persistent in encouraging me to try-out, I continued to resist. But one day, I remembered that talk that I had with Darryl. "You're a football player!" "Earl Campbell, Larry Csonka-type dude!"

"You're built like a Fullback!" Those words echoed in my head. It was time to give football a try.

My friends usually boasted about how much fun they had playing football. But they also warned me about a period of practice called "Hell Week." Hell week was actually two weeks of intense, physical conditioning. Two practices a day, six days a week, for a two-week period. "Can't be that bad," I thought. I quit after the first morning practice! Hell week?!? Aw, hell naw! Basketball practice could be tough, but this shit was insane! I never ran so much in my life! I saw kids throwing up and passing out on the field. And the coaches were like fucking drill sergeants! "What the fuck is this, the army?" I thought to myself. Even though I was warned about the intensity of hell week, I really didn't expect it to be THAT intense. Intimidated by my first, official experience with organized football, I decided to throw in the towel.

One of the assistant coaches noticed that I hadn't been to practice in a few days and asked some of my friends on the team to get me back to practice. Looking back, I am so glad that those guys encouraged me to go back to practice. The assistant coach talked me into returning and re-committing myself to the team. Having my position coach recognize my athletic ability and encourage me to seek out my full potential was a big confidence booster. I don't remember that particular coach's name, but I appreciate you and I am forever grateful. I trust that he has lived a blessed life.

As I struggled to learn football lingo and to keep up with the conditioning, I began to perform the drills with more confidence and fluidity. I became more confident, displaying my agility, quickness and strength.

Larry "Tank" Perdue

As each day went by, I found myself getting better. I became more competitive and more aggressive. In the weight room, I realized that I was stronger than the kids in my class, and just as strong, if not stronger than most of the upperclassmen. I began to earn respect from my teammates and coaches. But the biggest indication that I had become one of the "better" players on the team, was that I had begun to get fussed out by the head coach.

Coach Lou Underwood was the definition of a "Throwback." An old school, hard as nails coach that took no shit from anybody. If the coach yelled at you during practice, that meant he liked you. If the coach said, "hell man, that's unacceptable!" "Take my shit off and get outta here!" Then he meant exactly what he said. Our team had a healthy fear of our coach. Something about coach Underwood exuded a father-like quality. But he also reminded me of the people that would tell me that I'm too short and too heavy to play basketball.

I followed Darryl's advice and tried out as a fullback. I fell in love with the position. I was built to be a

FULLBACK

fullback. Football practice and workouts were turning fat into muscle, and my friends were noticing the physical change, as well. In practice, I learned how to run the ball hard and fast. I developed a spin move that I used upon contact that made it difficult to tackle me. My teammates gave me nicknames like "Stump" and "Bull", nicknames that described my stocky stature, toughness and athletic ability. Although I was showing a lot of promise, coach Underwood had his doubts about me playing in the backfield. Coach Underwood would often question if I was fast enough, or too big to be in the backfield. Going into my sophomore year, I was 5 foot four and weighed 203 lbs. On paper it looks bad, but in person I was becoming more muscular. But no matter how much the coach would yell, "he's too big!", or "he ain't fast enough to run that play!", he never took me out of the running backs unit. As each day of practice went by, I got better. When the JV team would scrimmage the Varsity, I would embarrass them. I would run them over. Truck them. Drag them 15-20 yards down the field. I would consistently punch it in during goal-line practice.

Sometimes I made mistakes that for sure would've had me kicked out of the backfield, like the time I knocked our QB's teeth out while receiving a hand-off during a drill. (Sorry, Alvin. Thanks for forgiving me. bro.) Coach was "foaming at the mouth" and was mad at me about that incident. Coach Underwood's threats to take me out of the backfield due to my weaknesses made me work harder in practice.

We are now quickly approaching the first day of school and summer practice is wrapping up. Time to hand out the game jerseys for week one of the football season. Coach Underwood chose which players made Varsity, and which players will play on the JV team. I got called into the locker room to receive my jersey, and I noticed that assistant coach Lindbergh had a Varsity jersey in his hand! Most kids would be excited, but not me. I didn't want to play Varsity football. Most of my friends were on the JV team. I told coach Lindbergh that I'd rather play on the JV team with my friends. Coach Lindbergh looked me in the eye, took a deep breath, and tore me a new asshole! "Lindburger", as we called him, was a large man with a sarcastic attitude. He could be funny but firm and was also a gym teacher at the school. Lindbergh stated to me that it was an honor to be chosen to play on the varsity team, and that I should play where coach Underwood wanted me to play, or don't play at all. Then he grabbed a JV jersey and tossed it to me. Number 35? What star fullback wore number 35? There weren't many that I knew of. I wanted a stud number, like 44 or 42. But Lindbergh wouldn't change my jersey number. He just stated that "numbers don't make the player, the player makes the number!" OK I get it. But I still wanted the jersey number I desired. I'm still a little salty about that, too. I was embarrassed by the chew-out, but happy to be playing football with my friends. After all, my friends were the reason I tried out for football in the first place.

So now it's week one of the JV football season, and I am about to play my first real football game. This ain't the kind of football that we played in the streets. I did not start the game at fullback. The JV coaches played two fullbacks before me. "This ain't fair," I thought. The coaches know that I am the best fullback on this team. Then late in the second quarter, I got my shot. Our offense had driven the ball into the red zone, but couldn't punch it in. The coaches called me in to run a dive on the goal line. The QB hikes the ball, I receive the hand-off and smack into the line hard and fast. I kept chopping my legs until I powered my way into the end zone. Touchdown! From that point on, I never came out of the game. I don't quite remember my stats, but I do remember having a few rushes for 10 or more yards. I scored our only TD and a two-point conversion. The game ended in a tie, the score 8-8.I earned a new kind of respect from my friends. Word got around school fast that I was a good football player. Dudes would ask if I really scored two touchdowns in the game (some people thought the two-point conversion run was also a TD run. Smh.) Girls that would usually laugh at me, were now giving me their phone numbers, and their attention. Even my teachers seemed to be genuinely proud of me and my performance. Wow! This feels great! Yeah, I think I like football. I can play this game.

FULLBACK

So now my confidence is through the roof. My teammates are stroking my ego and my coaches are giving me more attention. I am now clearly the starting fullback on the JV team. However, after week 3, my JV football season came to an abrupt end. I channeled all of my focus on football but slacked off in the classroom. My laziness and disinterest in completing my assignments ultimately led to my failure to meet the academic requirements to remain eligible to play. Simply put, I fucked up. It wasn't like the assignments were too hard or too complicated for my comprehension, I was just lazy, academically. Teachers would often tell me that I'm a smart kid, I'm just lazy. And that was true. I was also worried about how coach Underwood would react. I had a very healthy fear of this man. Coach Lou Underwood stood about 6' 2, maybe 6'3 and like I said before, he was no joke. He had a big, intimidating presence about himself that spoke volumes. Underwood had a reputation around the school as being one of the teachers that you better not try, because he wasn't scared and he didn't play games. Disrespect coach

Underwood and he would yoke your ass up quick! Coach had a well-known phrase that was an indicator of how serious he was. "Hell man, hell!" "that's unacceptable!" Those words were written on the boys and girls locker room doors and on many lockers. Some kids may have written his "catch-phrase" all over the campus to mock coach Underwood, but one thing that's for sure, we all knew that the graffiti was a sign of respect. Underwood often reminded us that he played college football for the late, great legendary coach Eddie Robinson, of Grambling State. He would tell us how tough it was to play for such a demanding coach and how important it was to hold each other accountable for our performances on the field. I feared coach Underwood, but I wanted to earn his respect and trust as a football player. Surprisingly, the coach didn't kick me off of the team, nor did he chew me out. He gave me a few words of encouragement, then said, "hell man, hell!" "You still gotta come to practice!"

It was very painful to watch our games from the sideline, but I learned a lot from watching and I readjusted my focus to the weight room. The short but sweet taste of success at the beginning of the season, left me fiending for more success playing football. I started to step up my effort in class. I vowed to myself that the only thing that can take me out of a game is injury, not ineligibility.

Some teammates began to organize off-season workouts not long after the football season ended. We would go to an area around the Rose Bowl, and run sprints up very steep hills, or hop the fence at John Muir high school and run drills on their football field. I became more interested in other players in the area and compared myself to other players that played my position. I was definitely impressed by a senior running back named Ricky Irvins, who played at John Muir high school. We would also find out where other local teams were conducting off-season workouts and go "scout" them. I studied Ricky, intensely. He was short and stocky, like me. But he was powerfully built and had "track" speed. He also ran on his schools' track team. He had legs like Earl Campbell and ran like Walter Payton. He even brushed waves in his hair! So did I!! (I used to have them spinnin", bro) Ricky just had all of the intangibles a natural running back has. Speed, quickness, agility, power, balance and a body built to give and take mighty blows. He ran the rock low and hard, and that's exactly how I wanted to run the rock. Low and hard.

April 1987, time for the football team's annual spring football camp. This is usually a non-contact camp, where most coaches would use this time for conditioning, refreshing skills and reviewing offensive and defensive schemes. I busted my ass during spring practice. I called out seniors and outperformed my position mates. I was noticeably becoming faster and stronger. Coach Underwood moved me defensively, from Defensive Tackle to Inside Linebacker. And I began to take the first team snaps for my positions, offensively and defensively. One day during the spring camp, Underwood walked through our warm-ups ranting and spewing statements of retribution for a lack of effort and energy. As he walked past me while I warmed up he quipped, "Perdue, you better have your damn grades right!" That was my official validation. I knew that I was going to be a beast on Varsity my junior year, and I think that coach knew it, too. John Muir HS football team had a different spring practice schedule than Marshall, so after our last practice of the spring camp, I went up to John Muir HS to watch Ricky Irvins practice. I wanted to get one last good look at Ricky. This dude looked awesome when he ran the ball in practice. He was heavily recruited going into his senior year, and John Muir had one of the premier programs in the area. Ricky would go on to star at the University of Southern California, and he also had a productive pro career in the NFL. As me and my homeboy Adrian began to walk home, I noticed a familiar looking man standing outside of the gate at the far end of the field. As we walked closer, I recognized that it was coach Underwood, out of all people! Before I could speak, coach said "you're up here watching Ricky, huh, Perdue?" I think coach appreciated my enthusiasm. He was surprised to see me there, but satisfied with the interest that I was showing.

It's the summer of 1987, and football camp is just around the corner. Some of my teammates and I had been working out together during the off-season. As a team, we were feeling very optimistic about the upcoming season. We talked trash to anybody that identified as a football player. We didn't care if guys' schools were on our schedule or not. We were loud-mouth, cocky and drunk from overconfidence. Everywhere we went, we made it known that the Marshall HS football team was in the house. Our football program didn't have a storied history. We weren't even recognized as being one of the top teams in our area. John Muir and Pasadena HS usually fought for the top spot every year, while schools like Marshall HS and Blair HS were always considered to have 2nd tier talent. But our class was just different. We knew we were going to be good. Very good. We had all of the elements that a good team could possess. We had speed, power, athleticism, and smart players at the most intricate positions. We also had great respect for our coaches, but most importantly, we all liked each other. We hung out together often, and truly had each other's backs. I think that in all sports, a winning season must begin with a winning attitude. And we definitely had a winning attitude, that's for sure. Shout out to the Marshall fundamental HS football team, class of 1989. You guys were some of the best friends I've ever had. May God bless you all.

Larry "Tank" Perdue

"Man Makes Plans, God laughs"

There's a saying that goes, "man makes plans, God laughs." I was told that this means that sometimes you can make plans and goals for yourself, but ultimately God will decide your fate. My mother and I moved from Milwaukee to California in search of a better life. If we would've stayed in Milwaukee, do I think we would've regressed or progressed? I don't know. But I did notice the hopelessness and unhappiness that began to consume my mother. And I know that we didn't move to California because she was chasing Robert. I think my mother was just fed up with struggling and wanted new opportunities, more than anything.

Unfortunately, we struggled in California too. We dealt with the same issues. A lack of financial resources and gainful employment, drug and alcohol abuse, and other situations that would drastically affect our family. My mother and her boyfriend Don had a reasonably good relationship. They had their ups and downs but appeared to be happy together. And I really liked Don. I thought he was a great guy. He opened his home to my mother and I, at a very crucial time in our lives, and I truly appreciate him. Unfortunately, drug and alcohol abuse would eventually tear my family apart, right before the start of summer football camp, going into my junior year. Our family problems got so bad that we had to leave Don's house.

My mother and I lived in a motel room while she and Don tried to work on their relationship. After a couple of weeks, they realized that their relationship was over. During this stressful time, I didn't attend summer football practice, which had started while I was consumed in all of this drama. I was basically looking after my mother and trying to survive during this most uncertain time of my life. We were eating bologna sandwiches living in a motel room wondering what's going to happen next. I notified coach Underwood about my situation. He expressed his empathy, and asked if I could live with my aunt, which really wasn't my real Aunt. She was Don's sister Gloria, no relation. And she was one of the reasons that my mother and Don fell out. We had no options. My mother had lost her job during the breakup, and we had no family or friends that would take us in. We were homeless. And on top of that, my grandmother, who lived in Chicago, had been planning a visit to California and was going to be in town soon.

My mother didn't inform my grandmother about our dire situation until she arrived. My grandmother was very disappointed and upset with us. After enjoying California for a few days, my grandmother bought us two one-way tickets to Chicago, and left out the next day. A few days later, we were on our way to Chicago to reside with my grandmother and family. This situation was killing me. I didn't even get a chance to say goodbye to all of my friends. I had just gotten used to living in California. I had endured all of the things that came with relocating to a new hood. Getting familiar with the area, meeting new friends and getting bullied by the resident thugs. The beautiful weather, pretty girls and tons of fun things to do, made it exceptionally different to me. I realized that my mom and I had actually found what we were looking for. A better quality of life. And for a few years we found just that, in California.

It's now mid-summer of 1987, entering my junior year in high school. Although I miss my friends and I'm agonizing over my missed opportunity to play football in California, I remained optimistic. I figured that some lucky high school in Chicago is about to get a beast of a fullback for their football team. My cousin Keith took me to the local Rec Center and introduced me to his friends. Some of the guys were my age, and they were cool. They accepted me right away. A couple of the guys played on their high school football teams and would often lift weights with me when we would meet up at the rec center. It was obvious that I was a football player. I was already stocky, but my body was beginning to develop definitive muscle. I also played a lot of basketball to pass the time every day. As a child growing up in Milwaukee, I used to visit Chicago at least twice a year. Chicago is only about 90 miles from Milwaukee, and the majority of my family lived in Chicago. I used to love to visit Chi-town when I was a kid. I would spend time with family on different sides of the city, and would have so much fun with my uncles and cousins. But Chicago wasn't Pasadena. I just didn't connect with people like I did in California. Besides hanging out at the rec center, there wasn't much to do.

It was time to find a school to attend, and there were three high schools in the area. I began to contact the head coach of each school and set up appointments to meet. Evanston township school was the first school that family and friends suggested I check out first. I was turned off and turned away by the head coach of Evanston high immediately. The coach asked me, "what position do you play?" "Fullback and Linebacker ", I responded. He laughed and said, "you're too short to play linebacker for me, and we have plenty of fullbacks, son. Thanks for coming". Then walked right out of the room. I thought to myself, wherever I land, I hope we play against that ass hole.

Sullivan high school was located just a few blocks away from the shabby apartment that my mother and I had just rented. Coach Pol appeared to be impressed when he met me. Coach Pol told me that his backfield was loaded, but he allowed all of his players opportunities to battle for positions. That's all I needed to hear. The word "opportunity". I knew that if I had a real shot at competing, I'd beat out the other chumps, convincingly. Still punch-drunk with confidence and determination, I decided to attend Sullivan high school and try-out for the football team.

During the first week of summer practice, I made my presence known. I displayed a ferocious attitude and intimidating swagger that intrigued the coaches and excited my teammates. I would lower my shoulders to run over and truck any fool that tried to tackle me. And boy o' boy did I love the contact! Ain't nothing like the sweet sound of shoulder pads and helmets colliding under brute force and high speeds! The sound echoes as it disappears into the atmosphere, leaving an indelible impression. Yeah man, in other words, it's a thing of beauty, baby. I worked hard and displayed my athletic ability in an effort to impress the coaches. The first people to recognize your talents aren't the coaches however, but the players. Your teammates are the guys that really experience and assess just how strong and fast you are through contact and competition. Of course coaches can make assessments based on performance, but your teammates actually experience your talent on another level. A lot of the guys on the team introduced themselves to me during breaks in practice. Most of them were impressed that I was from California, even teased me for moving back to the cold, snowy Midwest. Some of the guys were not as accepting and welcoming. I would just make note of the guys that chose to be assholes, and I would try to hit them in practice. Back then, we ran a lot of one-on-one drills like the Oklahoma drill or the hamburger drill, or Bull in the ring. These drills put a major emphasis on toughness and true grit. Some guys lost their respect after these drills, even their position and status on the team. I LOVED that shit! I feared no man and held my own and rather decisively. By the end of the first week of practice, I had earned a new nickname. Coach Pol began to call me "bowling ball". He stated that I would hit the hole so hard that bodies got knocked around like bowling pins when I ran the football. "You're just a big, black bowling ball!", he would yell. And of course, I ate it all up. Coaches and teammates praised my toughness and effort, and even though life at home wasn't all that great, at least the football gods were beginning to smile down on me.

Although I was seriously missing my friends in California, I was finally beginning to acclimate myself to the windy city. I believed that football could help me make the transition. But heartbreak and disappointment would give me another beatdown. After busting my ass during summer practice, taking snaps from the starters and outperforming most of the running backs, I barely played in a pre-season scrimmage with a local catholic school team. I didn't expect to start, but I took a lot of the first team snaps in practice, which is usually an indication that you're going to play. The next Monday before practice, I asked coach Pol about my "opportunity" to battle for my position. I stated that I'm sure that I'm just as good, if not better than the guys that he had played ahead of me at the scrimmage. Coach Pol stated that he has a senior running back that deserves his starting spot, simply because he has played for him since he was a freshman. He stated that this kid had taken a lot of punishment running the ball for him, and he has earned his starting spot through seniorship. Coach Pol also stated that he has two RBs that transferred from schools that played in Chicago's catholic league which was nationally recognized and revered. "So what happened to the opportunity to earn a starting position?" I said. Coach Pol responded with, "you're only a junior. You'll have plenty of opportunities to compete as the season progresses. But for now, it is what it is." Fucking liar! I felt betrayed by Coach Pol. "Man, fuck coach Pol and fuck this team! I'm not riding the pine for nobody! I'm better than the guys that played ahead of me, and everybody knew it. I can't trust this coach, I thought. I must find a new school to play football.

The first day of school, which would be the beginning of my junior year, was about a week away and I hadn't actually registered to attend Sullivan at that time. Amundsen high school was the third school on my

FULLBACK

list that I had planned to contact regarding their football program. Unfortunately, I forgot the name of the head football coach at Amundsen in 1987-88, but this man was truly unforgettable. He was a former army drill sergeant, and his voice had a command that would make the devil stand at attention. The coach at Amundsen was honest and truthful with me. He told me that he already had a fullback that he was expecting to have a great season, but he was a senior. The coach told me that if I came to play for Amundsen my junior year, that I could try out for any damn position I wanted to next year. I didn't take his statement literally, I just figured that he was trying to emphasize the fact that he was going to give me a great opportunity to be a big contributor to the team, my senior season. After my meeting with the coach, I met some of the Amundsen high school players. Not really a bunch of guys I would usually hang out with, I assumed. These guys were an eclectic group of guys, but they seemed, and turned out to be very cool. The next day I was at Amundsen high school practicing with the football team.

So once again, I immediately began to establish myself. On offense, I learned plays quickly and busted my ass on the practice field. Everything I did was with malicious intent. I went hard during every drill, whether contact or non-contact. The "bowling ball" was rolling again! I ran the rock with reckless abandon. I was already built low to the ground, with my short, stocky stature. This allowed me to enjoy an advantage of leverage especially versus taller players. I would also lay blocks on guys like a big, nasty offensive guard. On defense, I used my strength and quickness to shoot gaps and make plays. The coaches continuously applauded my effort and tenacity. My new teammates were also impressed, as they complimented me for my toughness and thirst for contact. Yep, I was beginning to feel myself again. "Fuck coach Pol!", I thought. "Fuck Sullivan!" I think I have found my new football home.

FULLBACK

Larry "Tank" Perdue

"It's a Cold World and Chicago is Colder"

I enrolled at Amundsen high school on the north side of Chicago and began my junior year of high school. On the first day of school, I quickly realized that I had made a bad decision. The hallways of Amundsen were run by Latino gangs and these dudes were very aggressive. I just moved from California, so the fact that these guys were Latino didn't bother me at all. There were more Latino gangs than black gangs in Cali, and back then, the two sides didn't clash often. In fact, I had plenty of Latino friends in California. But Amundsen was more like my first day of prison, than the first day of school. And like I said before, it was very clear that the Kings and Cobras controlled the school yard, respectively. But I wasn't struck with fear, just surprised at how this big, beautiful school could be so ghetto. I ignored all of the dudes flashing gang signs at me as I walked through the halls looking for my classrooms. I just moved from Cali, this gang shit ain't new to me. Don't fuck with me, and I won't fuck you up, was my mindset. I was short, but the weightlifting and training was starting to show. And I already had a natural mean-mug. I wasn't scared of anybody. I fought all the time growing up and had no problem throwing these hands. I wasn't worried about nothin', bro.

Now I'm well into my second week of practice with my new team, and I am proving myself to be a "dawg" out there on the practice field. The defensive coaches began to give me snaps with the first team defense as a "loop tackle", in our 5-2 defensive scheme. While things on the practice field are going well, things in the schoolhouse are not going so well. Some of these gang-banging fools are starting to test me. The only friends I had at the school were on the football team, and I usually didn't see those guys until practice, which is at the end of the day. I didn't have many classes with teammates either. I think most of the gangsters thought I was an "opp", because I kept mostly to myself, I didn't have a lot of friends. That kind of reclusive-like attitude and awareness makes dudes think that you have something to hide, like what side (of town) are you from?

Or, who do you ride with? Peoples or folks? And to make matters worse, I just wasn't feeling the school! Most of my classmates were click-ish and corny. I wasn't happy at Amundsen, and it became a battle with-in to drag myself out of bed every morning and go to school.

Friday. Game day. It's week two of the football season at Amundsen high. We were playing Slinger high school. Slinger had this tall, skinny kid at running back, and he was killing us. Slinger's offense continuously ran sweeps and dives, and this kid was definitely eatin'. Coach began to rotate me into the game with the first team loop tackle. When I was in the game on defense, I used my strength and quickness to shoot gaps and make plays or stand my ground so that our linebackers could flow to the ball. Our defense began to hold Slinger's offense in check, but our offense, which lost our starting QB in the 2nd quarter to injury, struggled. We couldn't score enough points to make up the deficit. We eventually lost the game. I don't remember the score, but I do remember how excited the defensive coaches were with my performance and effort. I was told right there on the field after the game that I would be the starting loop tackle on our defensive unit. Unashamedly, I didn't care about the loss, and I was satisfied with my performance on defense. But I had a burning desire to run the rock, man! I would observe the starting full back in practice, and I knew that I was a better full back. He was a big, heavy kid, but he wasn't really quick, and he ran upright. "Just a big, moving target.", I thought to myself. I ran the ball in practice like a scud missile! Teammates often commented about how difficult it could be to tackle me in practice. I was pretty sure that the starting fullback job would be mine my senior year, but I wasn't sure if I could continue to tolerate attending this thug-haven of a school.

Not even 3 weeks into the start of the school year, the shit is about to hit the fan. One of the Latin Kings decided to "skip" me in the lunch line in the school cafeteria. Before I could say "excuse me", this dude turned around, got in my face and said, "man, fuck you! What, you mad?' And all of a sudden, we're surrounded by all of his buddies. In most of the neighborhoods that

I've grown up in, getting jumped was kind of like an inevitable passage to manhood. At some point you're going to get jumped for something. Robbed. Gang-banged. Messed with the wrong girl. It all comes with the territory. I've been threatened by dudes with gangster-ish reputations before, and one thing that I've learned is that you never show fear. There is a saying that goes, "weakness is fear leaving the body." And trust me, if real gangsters can smell your fear, they will eat you alive. So now here I am, by myself, about to get jumped in my new school's cafeteria. I responded to "super thug". I said, "Man, you need all these niggas to help you skip in line? If you're that damn hungry, you can HAVE my spot, bro." Some of dude's guys thought what I said was funny. Then school security came in like they were breaking up a prison riot. After that incident, the mean-mugging and intimidating, aggressive behavior from random dudes escalated. I knew that very soon, I was going to have to fight and defend myself. But that was the problem. I was by myself in a school crawling with gangs. At practice one day, my teammates told me that some of the Kings were talking about jumping the "little swole football dude", because I lived in one of their rivals' hoods. First of all, I didn't even know anybody on my block in Chicago. I barely saw kids my age around my aunt's apartment, nor did I see many kids on my block. I'm sure those guys wouldn't have given a fuck anyway.

It's Friday. Game time, the third game of the season. I'm not 100% sure, but I think we played Senn high school. I didn't have an all-star performance, but I did make a few big plays and held my own against some pretty big, strong guys on that Senn team. We lost that game too, but I was playing with a chip on my shoulder, and my defensive coaches loved it. But I still yearned to play the position that I was born to play. I was built to rush the rock with violent intentions. I ain't no defensive lineman, I'm a fullback! Give me the ball!

Later that night, after the game while walking to the bus stop, a car full of dudes drove past me yelling profanities and throwing up gang signs with their fingers. I remembered my teammates warning me of a rumor that I was going to get jumped. I began to look for anything on the ground that I can use as a weapon. I walked past a garbage bin that had broken chair pieces on top of it. I grabbed a broken chair leg and proceeded to the bus stop. I was ready to accept an ass whuppin', but before I get stomped, somebody is gonna eat this wood, bro! So now I'm walking to the bus stop, tired and sore, clenching my book bag in one hand and a broken chair leg in the other hand. I was scared. But I had nowhere to run, nowhere to hide and nobody to help me fight these dudes. I don't even know why these dudes keep fucking with me! I don't gangbang, and I don't think I tried to pull one of their girlfriends. I just couldn't understand why they wanted to get me so bad. I made it to the bus stop, now if only this slow ass bus would hurry up and come before that car rolled up on me again, I'll be safe. Damn. Here comes that car again. The same car full of Kings pulled up on me displaying the same aggressive, intimidating behavior. Then some fool in the back seat leans out of the window and throws a 40-ounce beer bottle at me. The punk ass coward missed. Another guy laughed and said, "is that stick for us, little bitch ass nigga?" "Bitch ass nigga, ill pop you right now!" Then he flashed a gun at me, and he and his merry band of idiots sped off, laughing and threatening me.

Like I said before, I was raised in the hood. I've been bullied by gang members before. And I have seen how brutal and vicious a gang beatdown can be. And I also had a keen sense of knowing when trouble is at its boiling point. The shit was about to get real; I could sense it.   I finally decided to inform my mother about the issues I was having at school. Momma was very concerned and strongly suggested that I transfer to another school. My mother didn't care if I played football or not, she just wanted me out of that school, immediately. Wow. All of that hustling to find a school and a coach that would give me an opportunity, only to end up back where I started from. So after about 4-5 weeks at Amundsen high, due to the harassment from gang bangers, I left the football team and transferred to Sullivan high school. It was the only school in the area with open seats. My guidance counselor happened to be, none other than, of course! The head football coach,

coach Pol. Coach Pol was a man of average stature. He didn't have the usual qualities of a coach that would stand out. He didn't have a commanding presence or a competitive zeal. He just seemed like an average guy. Coach Pol wasn't surprised to see me again. He stated that he knew I wouldn't be successful finding a school to play at and start for, because summer camps were almost over when I left. He stated that most coaches pretty much had their roster spots decided by then. He also stated that I should've been patient and just stayed with the team. But I wasn't comfortable playing for a coach that's not completely honest and sincere. Coach Pol stated that if I'm interested in playing football I could return to the team as an offensive guard. I felt that he was adding "insult to injury", so to speak." I'm not going to block for dudes that can't run the rock better than me", I thought. Coach Pol was trying to be cute. What an asshole! My ego wouldn't allow me to accept coach Pol's offer. I refused to play on coach Pol's offensive line, but also refused to give up my dream of playing football.

FULLBACK

Larry "Tank" Perdue

"Milwaukee, I'm Home!"

In high school, my ultimate goal was to earn a scholarship and play college football. Without a high school football team to play for, that goal was all but dead. But I didn't give up on achieving that goal. I figured that if I worked out as much as possible, I could still be in shape to try-out for any college that I may attend. I was naive, of course. I had no knowledge of the policies, procedures and politics of college football. So here I am Stuck living in a place that I don't wanna be and attending yet another "thug-trap" of a school. And worst of all, I'm not playing football! How depressed can a 16–17-year-old kid become? Well, just when I thought that my life couldn't get any more complicated than it was, it became more complicated.

So as I began to acclimate myself as a student at Sullivan high school, I experienced the same issues that I had to address at Amundsen high school. Gang banging bullies and stuck-up girls. Each day began to be more depressing than the last. My home life was even more troubling. As I mentioned earlier, my mother and I moved into a dingy, one bedroom apartment with nothing but the clothes on our backs, on the north side of Chicago. We had no furniture, just a raggedy, old 18-inch color TV. We slept on the floor in the living room because that was the warmest room in a poorly heated apartment. My mom did the best she could with what little she had. She had just landed a job as a nursing assistant and was working 2nd and 3rd shifts. My mother worked very hard to keep a roof over me, my brother and my sisters' heads. When I think about the resilience and strength that was required to overcome my most difficult battles, I also think about my mother. One night, my mother was stricken suddenly by a brain aneurysm as she rode the bus home from work. Although she was suffering through a traumatic medical event, she still managed to get off of the bus and walk to my cousin's apartment (which was 2 blocks away from the bus stop). My mother was a woman of incredible inner strength. She would later successfully complete therapy, regain full use of her faculties and enjoy the remaining years of her life. During her time of recovery however, we were unable to pay rent and were facing eviction. My grandmother, who blamed me for our unfortunate situation in California, offered my mother a place to stay and to continue to recover. But not me. Boobie had to go somewhere else. She stated that she didn't have enough room for me, but we knew that wasn't true. My grandparents' house had a huge, insulated and carpeted basement that my uncle had all to himself. Of course, that didn't matter. It was clear that my grandmother didn't want me in her house. I had to find somewhere to live, and fast. My mother contacted my father, who lived in Milwaukee and made him aware of our situation. My father reluctantly agreed to let me come live with him and his girlfriend's family. This move would be temporary, until my mother was healthy enough to re-assume caring for herself. Boom! Another devastating blow to my life! On the move again! At Least my mother will have the opportunity to heal in a more comfortable, peaceful environment, with family members that will love and support her. I, on the other hand, was headed back to Milwaukee. My travels have come full circle now. When I lived in California, I always wished that I could go back to Milwaukee, for some reason. Even well after I had acclimated myself to the "California lifestyle." I always wanted to go back. Be careful what you wish for.

I stepped off of the greyhound bus with a bag that had 3, maybe 4 outfits and a few pairs of underwear. My father, along with his girlfriend Diane and her two kids, April and Steven, received me with open arms. Although I was saddened by the separation from my mother, I looked at my re-location as yet another opportunity to play football again. It's almost the second semester of my junior year in high school, and I had to find a school to enroll at, immediately. According to Milwaukee Public School policy, I had to go to a school in my residential area. The only school in my area that had openings was Washington high school. Washington was a big school with a lot of students. I knew a few kids from elementary school, and a few kids from old neighborhoods that I've lived in. So that made my transition easier. After I received my student ID, class schedule and locker number, I asked my student escort to take me to meet the head football coach. The escort took me to coach Lehman's Office. My first impression of coach Lehman is that he resembled a basketball coach. He was tall with an athletic build. During my brief meeting with Lehman, He appeared to be a pretty cool guy. We discussed my football journey and he appeared to be understanding and empathetic. Coach Lehman told me that he would love to give me a shot to compete. Lehman stated that the weight room was open every day after school, and that's where I would meet most of the kids on the football team. Coach Lehman also made me aware of an upcoming skills camp sponsored by the Wisconsin Badgers football program, which I was definitely interested in attending. This is exactly what I wanted! I just wanted a fair shot to compete for my position, fullback. No favoritism, no lies, just an honest opportunity. So now my confidence is back, and I have a renewed purpose in life. I can focus on playing football again!

FULLBACK

I am now beginning to acclimate myself to yet another school. Things ain't all that great, but things ain't all that bad either. I miss my mother dearly, but I was definitely more comfortable living and attending school in Milwaukee than in Chicago. We kept in touch often, As she continued to recover from the effects of the brain aneurysm and the surgeries that followed. I survived a lot of tough times with my mother. Through thick and thin, she never abandoned me. She kept me right by her side through it all. I knew that if there was anyone in this world that really loved me, it was my mother. I stayed optimistic that she would make a full recovery and we would be back together again. Considering the circumstances, I now have a chance to build on the relationship between my father and I. When we moved to California, I had very little contact with my father, which was really hard to deal with. I really could've used his guidance and direction at that time. Now I was living under the same roof as my father, which I could only dream about as a kid.

Larry "Tank" Perdue

My father was married to another woman when he was dating my mother. My mother stated to me that she didn't know that (LC, my dad's name) was married until after he impregnated her. My father had a whole 'nother family on the other side of town. But he still made his presence felt in my life. Daddy would pick me up on weekends and take me to get haircuts, new shoes and of course, a Big Mac from McDonalds! He wasn't the most consistent guy, but I appreciate the times that he shared with me as a kid. Unfortunately, our father-son relationship didn't really thrive during my stay with him. My father had grown sullen in his ways and didn't have the energy or interest to be an "involved" father. He was a slave to his routine. Monday through Thursday, my dad was up and out of the door to work at 5:30 am, and back home and in bed by 6:30 pm. Friday nights and Saturdays were his time to unwind from a long, hard work week and get "out and about" in the city. We didn't spend any quality time with each other. The fact that my father struggled with alcohol abuse didn't help much either. He was there physically but mentally he checked out on me.

FULLBACK

My junior year at Washington high school has come to an end, and I have earned a reputation for being one of the strongest dudes in the weight room. A lot of the guys thought that was particularly impressive because of my stature. I never really had that growth spurt that I was expecting. At the end of my junior year in high school, my height was measured 5 feet 6 inches (without shoes on, lol!) and I weighed 217 pounds. Kinda heavy to be so slight of height, but I was still very quick and agile. Before summer practice began, coach Lehman took a group of players to the Dial camp. This was the football camp that Lehman had mentioned earlier. I had a great performance at the camp. The facilitating coaches continuously gave me high praise during drills. The coaches acknowledged my effort and abilities, which boosted my confidence through the roof! I also observed how my competition performed at the camp. I believed that I measured up very well with the other running backs at the Dial camp, and I also believed that I had outperformed the other fullbacks that were on my high school's team. Coach Lehman told me that I looked good at the camp, and that I should make sure I continued to work out until the start of summer practice. On the bus ride home from the football camp, I could barely contain my excitement! I was so glad to be playing football again.

FULLBACK

Larry "Tank" Perdue

"She Keeps Breaking My Heart"

It's now July of 1988, and it's the first day of summer football practice at Washington high. I've been waiting for this day all summer. For weeks I'd been begging my father to buy me a pair of cleats and other items I needed for football practice. Dad would just brush me off. "Don't worry about it, I'll take care of it." he would say. My father never bought the cleats. So now I have to practice wearing a pair of old, worn-out top ten Adidas basketball shoes. These were the only pair of shoes I had. And to make matters worse, it rained on the first day of practice. I asked around the locker room if anyone had an extra pair of cleats. Most of the guys said no, some even laughed and got on my case for not being prepared and too broke to afford a pair of cleats. But I didn't let their ignorance discourage me. I just had to make do with what I had. So much for good ol' optimism! I had a terrible practice! I had absolutely no traction on the wet grass field. I was constantly slipping, tripping and falling during drills due to poor footing. The assistant coaches noticed that I had on inappropriate shoes and barked at me for being unprepared for practice. I was frustrated, but I continued to work hard and finish practice. I went home determined to find a pair of cleats for the next day of practice.

Domestically, my life had been fairly stable since my return to Milwaukee. But my life with my father would be short-lived. My Dad and his girlfriend had what appeared to be a great relationship when they were sober, and a not-so-great relationship when they would drink. They both struggled with alcohol abuse, and at times their breakdowns in communication would end up in physical confrontations. Other than the occasional skirmish, everything appeared to be just fine. But later on that day after practice, my father came into my room and told me to call my sister. "Why?", I asked. "Cuz we gotta go, we gotta leave. You gotta go live with Charlotte." Dad responded. My sister Charlotte had just moved into a 3-bedroom apartment with a friend and 4 children. "What happened? What did I do?" I thought to myself. All I knew is that Dad was packing up his stuff and he made me pack up my stuff too. Damn! I'm on the move again! My father drove me to my sister's apartment and told me that he'd come see me soon. I asked him why did we have to leave Diane's house, and he stated, "cuz it was just time to go, Boobie. Diane and I aren't together anymore. Then Dad said, "you'll be ok over here with your sister." "I'll be checkin' up on you." Then drove away. Wow. Another sudden relocation without an explanation. And to my surprise, I learned that my father moved back in with Diane just a couple of days after WE had gotten thrown out of her house. Obviously, I wasn't invited back. My sister welcomed me into her home with open arms, but it was obvious that she wasn't exactly happy about the situation. And I still was determined to find a pair of cleats to wear at practice the next day. I desperately reached out to every family member and friend that I could contact. I even called my mother and asked if anyone at my grandmother's home could wire me money to buy football cleats. I knew it would crush her if she couldn't help me, and I really tried to resist calling her. But I was desperate. After learning about my situation, my mother was very disappointed with my father. Unfortunately, I wasn't able to buy or borrow a pair of cleats to wear at the next days' practice.

The next day I arrived to practice early, and asked coach Lehman if there were any old pairs of cleats left behind from former players that I could wear to practice. Lehman reached behind his desk and handed me a box of miscellaneous football gear. Old neck rolls, mismatched thigh and knee pads, broken straps and belts, and a few pairs of well-worn cleats. My eyes lit up and I immediately grabbed the cleats out of the box. "Thanks coach!" I yelled as I hustled to my locker to get dressed for practice. When I began to decide which pair of cleats to wear, I noticed that the shoes were all mismatched! Aww man! As frustration began to build, I found two shoes that actually matched. They were an old, worn-out pair of Astro turf shoes, and they were size 12s. I wore a size 10 and ½ shoe. But these well used Astro turf shoes were better than my old top tens, I figured.

Larry "Tank" Perdue

I had a much better performance in practice even though I still struggled with poor footing due to the old, worn out Astro turf shoes. A proper pair of football cleats are very important to a football player. Football is often a game of leverage, and you must be able to sustain core ability and balance when physically engaged. A players' ability to accelerate, stop on a dime and quickly change direction can determine their success on the field. After that second practice of the football camp ended, Lehman pulled me aside. He told me to go work with the offensive line at tomorrow's practice. Stunned, I asked, "why?". Lehman stated that I would never be more than a 2nd or 3rd string fullback on his team. He stated that I would have a more favorable opportunity to start on the O-line, than in the backfield. Most guys would have probably accepted the position change, But I knew what position I was destined to play on the football gridiron. "What about the Dial camp?" I said. Hoping that he hadn't forgotten how well I performed. "I dunno. You seemed quicker at the camp." Lehman said. "It's the shoes coach! I need cleats!" I responded. But Lehman disregarded that fact. He just reinforced his encouragement to practice with the O-line. I walked to the locker room stunned and crushed. Damn! If only I had some damn cleats! I couldn't believe that coach Lehman had lost confidence in me that quick. I thought about how embarrassed I would be at practice the next day. I felt that the position change was a demotion. It would tell other players that I wasn't athletic enough to play the fullback position. I knew that deep down in my soul, I can play fullback at any football program, I just needed a real opportunity. As I got dressed at my locker, frustration turned into anger. "Fuck Lehman!", I thought. "Another asshole coach playing games with my career!", I said to myself. On the bus ride home from practice, I made the decision to quit the Washington high school football team. I'd rather not play at all than be humiliated by an ignorant coach.

As I was preparing for summer football practice at Washington, I had also enrolled to attend summer school at Marshall high school. My series of school transfers due to my situations of displacement, made it complicated to determine if I was eligible to meet Milwaukee Public Schools' academic requirements. MPS determined that I needed two credits to be classified a 12th grader or senior. My plan was to attend and complete the summer session at Marshall, and to continue to attend the upcoming regular school year at Washington. But at this point, I was tired of chasing the dream, and I just wanted to graduate. As much as I loved the sport of football, it just kept breaking my heart. I was tired of being frustrated and disappointed. It was time to leave that chick (football) alone, man.

FULLBACK

Larry "Tank" Perdue

"When Tank Met Jerry"

I had just quit the Washington high school football team, maybe a week or two before the summer school session began. During this "down-time", I would go hang out with friends from old neighborhoods that I used to live in as a kid. One day, while hanging out on 36th street with some friends, a car pulls up, and a guy leans out of the rear window and says, "Hey dawg, I got yo' twin in the back seat!" Then a guy steps out of the car and walks over to me. As he approached, I immediately realized why the dude said he had my twin in the back seat. This dude was built just like me. He was about my skin tone and was just as stocky and muscular. Everybody laughed in astonishment at how similar we looked. For some reason, our friends encouraged us to engage in a foot race, in the middle of the street. Our friends called the markers. From the big tree in front of Mrs. Anderson's house, to the light pole in front of Marty's house. OK, let's go! I was very confident and felt that I could win the race. I could see that my "opponent" had a competitor's edge about himself, as well. So we lined up side by side, and....go! As we took off, I could hear our friends explode with excitement over how quick we were! Halfway through the race he began to pull away from me, but only by a step. I usually gained speed on the back end when I would sprint, but I couldn't close that one step gap that dude had on me. My "twin" won the race. He beat me by a nose. After the race, my twin asked if I played football. I explained the situation that I had at Washington high school and stated that I was done with football. "Twin" told me that he was the starting fullback at Marshall high school, and that I should come play ball with him. That's ironic, I thought. This dude looks like me, and he plays the same position that I have struggled to play my entire high school career. And he's asking me to transfer to Marshall, to play and possibly compete for the same position. This dude is really cool, but he's pretty cocky as well, I thought. I told my "twin" that I was attending summer school at Marshall, and I would consider it. Although we had a rather random introduction, I felt a genuine connection to that dude, big Jerry Baskin.

So now I'm attending summer school at Marshall high, and I've been hanging out with Jerry who was becoming more influential in convincing me to transfer to Marshall my senior year. In 1988, Milwaukee Public Schools did not require student/athletes to sit out a year of athletic competition after transferring from another school. I couldn't ignore the fact that I still had an urge to play football, but I had reservations. I was really fed up with the politics of football and dealing with ignorant coaches. But after attending just a week of summer school at Marshall high, I was sold! Man, summer school at Marshall in 1988 was loads of fun! The kids seemed to be more friendly and social. My classes were actually interesting and exciting. I was enjoying summer school so much that I decided to transfer from Washington high and complete my senior year at Marshall high. I had also decided to try my hand at football again. Why not, I figured. The school feels right. I know that Jerry is the starting fullback on the team, and that could be a problem for me. but we had talked about being in the backfield together, which could've been a possibility. I needed to speak to the head coach.

As summer school was wrapping up, football practice at Marshall had just begun. I asked a classmate from one of my summer school classes, who happened to be on the football team, to introduce me to the coach. Jerry Golembiewski is a Wisconsin Hall of Fame high school football coach. He's won a lot of games during his coaching career. Coach "Go-Go", appeared to be excited to meet me. He stated that he had heard about me from various players on the team. I had worked out at Marshall's open weight room during the summer school session where I had previously met a lot of the guys on the team. I explained my situation at Washington high, and Go-Go appeared to be empathetic. He stated that I had a lot of competition in the backfield but he would love to see me compete against Jerry for the starting fullback job. I wasn't happy with having to compete with Jerry. Jerry and I had become really cool and I knew that camp battles could turn friends into foes. Jerry also had advantages. It was clear that he was a "coach favorite" as he had often gone out for lunch or ice cream with Go-Go's wife. Jerry was also the incumbent. He was the starting fullback the previous season and Go-Go had big expectations for the 5'8, 240 lb. junior running back. I've seen this kind of favoritism before, and I knew I had a snowball's chance in hell to win the starting fullback spot. But I figured that Go-Go would have to just find a way to get us both on the field. We both were equally talented and had similar measurements. We were both short, stocky and built to bang. Both of us we're quick, agile and we were hogs in the weight room. Our most competitive face-offs came under the bar. We had a great assistant coach that pushed us to get stronger every day. Before I continue, I must pay homage to good ol' coach Rupert, affectionately known as "Roop." This man was a character that even Mark Twain couldn't create. Like Jerry and I, Roop was a short but large guy. He was a hard-core weightlifter, who on occasion would wrestle bears at festivals up north in Wisconsin. (Roop actually showed us photos of him grappling with a young, muzzled and declawed black bear in 1989.) Roop was a great motivator, and he taught us weight training tips that I still use to this day. I don't think anyone enjoyed the rivalry between Jerry and I more than Roop.

It's now about 2-3 weeks into practice and I am again earning the respect of my teammates and coaches. Can you believe that I still didn't have a decent pair of cleats, before I began to practice with the team? This time I was lucky. I borrowed an unused pair from a teammate. They were some old, worn-out white Nikes with a blue Nike check on the side. Size 10 and ½, perfect! Jerry had become preoccupied with things outside of football and was appearing to regress in both his potential and his commitment. Jerry was my guy, but it was obvious that I was outperforming him in practice. Go-Go also noticed Jerry's regression and began to give me more snaps in practice. I embraced the opportunities and continued to work hard not realizing the new threat to me winning the starting fullback position.

Underwood was a tall, white kid with long blonde hair and blue eyes. It was ironic to me that he shared the same last name as my former coach in California. He was our version of that kid "Sunshine", from the movie "Remember the Titans", long before the film came out. Underwood was also having an impressive summer football camp, catching the eyes of coach Golembiewski. But Underwood also had a problem with totally committing to the team. Underwood would miss practice often. Sometimes he came to practice with liquor on his breath. But he was a really cool dude, man. We all loved him. He had a great personality and busted his ass in practice, when he decided to come. But I felt that I was also outperforming Underwood and that I had displayed more of a commitment to the team. As Go-Go continued to lose confidence in Jerry he began to work Underwood and I in with the first team offense in practice. I thought that now the real battle is between Underwood and I. I believed that I had an advantage over Underwood. He wasn't the fastest or strongest fullback I've seen, but he could break a tackle and haul off for big runs in practice. But I was doing the same things in practice too. Only I ran the rock more violently.

FULLBACK

The summer break is coming to an end, and I am excited to begin my senior year at Milwaukee Marshall. I felt good about my work ethic and performance at football practice and was expecting to play a significant role on the team. Even though I hadn't officially earned the starting fullback position that I coveted so dearly, I was satisfied with how things were working out.

Larry "Tank" Perdue

"Once an Eagle, Always an Eagle"

It's the first game of the season, which is now my senior year of high school. We're playing at Riverside high school. This is it. I still had a chance to get on the field, make plays and garner some attention from some college programs. At this point it didn't matter to me which division level of football I played in college. I just wanted to play college football anywhere that would accept me. In 1988-89, it was much more difficult to contact or have access to college coaches than it is today. Nowadays, student/athletes have tools like HUDL, where they can make video clips of their performances accessible to anybody. But even if I had HUDL back then, I didn't have any game footage to present to coaches. I've spent my entire high school career on the run. Running from homelessness, running from violence and running from failure and disappointment. I didn't play anywhere long enough to earn attention. But now it seems like I'm going to get the opportunity that I always wanted. During the 3rd quarter of the game, I realized that I haven't received any "tick" (playing time") at fullback. Jerry was having an average game, but Underwood had made a few plays, by breaking a few carries for big yards. I played in a 3 man rotation at defensive tackle all game, and I was still waiting to get my shot on offense. "Here we go again", I thought to myself. Another coach that's full of shit. I proved that I'm the best fullback of the bunch! I worked harder than those guys worked! I came to practice every day, unlike those guys. I ran the rock like a Tank during our annual 4-team summer scrimmage, and during all of summer camp. I was so pissed that I wouldn't talk to Jerry or Underwood on the sidelines, as if it was their fault that Go-Go didn't play me on offense. Late in the 4th quarter, with the game already decided, (we lost) coach Go-Go put me in the game at fullback, and called a fullback dive. As soon as the ball was snapped, our O-line collapsed, and I barely received the hand -off before being tackled for a loss by Riverside's defense. I was crushed. Our O-line had completely given up and accepted their ass whipping with a Coke and a smile. On our last offensive series of the game, Go-Go called "fullback belly right". I had another shot at making a big play. But of course, with the game pretty much being over, and my O-line pretty much having checked out, it was another useless carry. After the game, as we headed through the tunnel on our way to the locker rooms, I heard a voice yell my name, "Perdue!" I looked up in the stands and kept walking. "Perdue!" I heard it again. It was coach Lehman, the football coach at Washington high school. He yelled out, "you're not playing, Perdue!" "What an asshole", I thought. Why is this grown ass man taking pleasure in seeing me fail to reach my goals? I was so shocked by his pettiness that I couldn't respond. Coaches are supposed to help raise your confidence, not crush it.

I went home that night extremely disappointed. We lost the first game of the season, and I hardly played in the backfield. The next week in practice, Go-Go put me on special teams. I took my helmet off and walked off the field. I was angry and heartbroken. Coaches usually put non-starting underclassmen on special teams. Starters were usually reserved from playing on special teams. I thought that being assigned to special teams was a sign that I was out of the loop at fullback. I walked off of the field and straight to the locker room. I sat down at my locker, and I cried. "I'm done with football", I thought. Then I quickly changed, walked to the bus stop and went home.

Just minutes after I arrived home, my sisters' apartment, I received a call from Diane, my fathers' girlfriend. Diane stated that "your football coach called over here and said to tell you that they have good intentions for you". Diane said that the coach requested that I come to his office before practice tomorrow. She also said that the coach sounded sincere and didn't want me to quit the team. I thanked Diane for giving me the message, and I assured her that I would talk to the coach.

The next day after school, and before football practice, I went to coach Golembiewskis office to talk. Go-Go asked me why I quit. I told him that I didn't get a fair shot at winning the fullback position. Go-Go stated that from his assessments in practice, he had decided that none of us would be considered the starting fullback. He stated that Jerry, Underwood nor I had "done enough" to really separate ourselves from each other. Go Go stated that he planned to have me in a rotation on both offense and defense. He also stated that I will become more involved in the offense as the season progresses. Our talk was positive and assuring. I figured that as long as I am given a shot at fullback, I'll play "balls to the wall" on both sides of the ball! My teammates accepted me back with open arms. They all were very supportive and encouraging. As I said before, your teammates are the guys that recognize your talents first. These guys had to tackle me in practice every day. They knew I had some "dawg" in me! It was just waiting to be unleashed!

If I recall correctly, Fort Atkinson high school was our next game. I played a lot of snaps on both sides of the ball during that game, and although I didn't get many carries at fullback, I had a good defensive game. Unfortunately, we lost that game, too. Go Go definitely kept his word of making me more involved in the overall game plan. But I still wanted more carries. I knew that I could help us win but I needed to run that rock, man.

As each day of practice went by, certain situations began to cause issues within our football team. Jerry and Underwood were still the main ball carriers on our team, but their personal issues were beginning to affect their commitments to the team. By the 3rd game of the season, Underwood had gotten himself into trouble, and was detained into a juvenile detention facility. Jerry began to miss practice more often, due to a demanding after school job that also contributed to excessive weight gain. These factors ultimately led to Go Go changing his position from fullback to offensive guard, later in the season. Go Go was sick of their excuses, and during practice of week 4, named me the starting fullback. I was excited and most of my teammates were happy for me. They all knew that I deserved the shot. I validated Go Go's decision by busting my ass in practice. But I soon realized that Go Go wasn't ready to let go of his love affair with Jerry. I was the starting fullback, but Jerry was still receiving the bulk of the carry load. Go Go still didn't have enough trust and confidence to make me the bell cow of the offense. And besides establishing myself as one of the best players on the team in practice, we were struggling to win games. Our frustration was boiling over, and we began to point fingers at each other. The finger-pointing eventually became fist fights and skirmishes inside and outside of the locker room. My frustration came to a boiling point in the weight room, one evening. Our star QB began to berate me about my lack of production on the field. He mentioned how I would be unstoppable in practice but didn't give the same effort in games. "Tank, you be killin' in practice but don't do shit in games". That comment really stunned and angered me. I threw a punch at him, but fortunately I missed, and the confrontation was quickly squashed. As I left the weight room, I slammed the doors to the gym so hard that I shattered the glass. Go-Go told me that I would have to pay to repair the doors. I never paid a cent for those damn doors.

As tensions grew in my football life, my home life wasn't faring any better. My sister and her friend weren't exactly a wholesome, melodic couple. What you may deem "domestic violence", they would probably say that they just "loved hard". Charlotte and Brenda didn't just fight when they had "bad disagreements", they had straight up brawls and battles. Nothing seemed to be off limits in a fight. A hot clothing iron, a small dumbbell, anything that could be weaponized, became a weapon. How could two people that claimed to love each other become so violent with each other? And why would they fight in front of the kids? Obviously, my sister and her friend had a very tumultuous relationship, which affected how I communicated with both of them. This living arrangement was dysfunctional, and I was ready to go. And they were ready for me to go, too. I came home from practice one night, opened my room door and found my mother sitting in a chair watching my TV!!! I was shocked and excited!!! I was extremely grateful to see my mother, but I also noticed that she hadn't fully recovered from the brain aneurysm, and I asked my mother," why did my grandmama send you to Milwaukee while it was obvious that you're still recovering?" I remember the sad, sorrowful look she gave me when she responded, "Don't be mad at your grandmother baby, it was time for me to go." I didn't agree with that. But I didn't press the issue. I was just happy to see my mother. I was a little frustrated with the fact that my grandmother didn't check to see what kind of environment she was sending my mother into. My mother wasn't naive, she could sense that Charlotte and Brenda's home wasn't a happy home. My mother had a lot of questions, and I gave her answers, the whole sobering truth of how the household was struggling. We had a long talk that night, and we decided to pursue housing for ourselves once she was awarded disability benefits. Unfortunately, our plans would get a swift kick in the butt. After sharing my room with my mother for a couple of weeks, I came home from practice one night, again, to a shocking surprise. I walked up the hallway stairs to our apartment and knocked on the door. One of the kids let me in. As I walked to my room, I noticed that something looked different about my room. As I walked into the room, Donnie, a relative of Brenda, stopped me at the door. Donnie stated to me that "you and your momma don't live here anymore, y'all staying with your auntie." Then he pointed to a garbage bag and said, "that's all your stuff right there." Suspiciously, Charlotte and Brenda were nowhere to be found. I needed details, like why is this happening? And exactly where is my mother? Which auntie? My mother had a few close friends that I called auntie. Donnie said that he was told to give me my bag and send me to Zippy's house. Ok great. At Least my mother is around loving caring friends that we considered family. Zippy and Katie took us in after we were unceremoniously kicked out of my sisters' house. Maintaining stable housing for my mother and I would prove to be an on-going struggle throughout my senior year of high school and beyond.

Larry "Tank" Perdue

"Was It Worth It?"

We're now approaching the last 4 games of the season, and although we were a below .500 team, we still had a slim chance of earning a berth in the Wisconsin state football play-offs. One day, right before practice began, Go Go summoned me to his office. He stated that coach Lehman called and said that I owed him football gear from when I attended Washington high school. Go Go stated that I would be ineligible to play our next game, unless I go to Washington and explain what happened to Lehman's football gear. I found it very ironic that coach Lehman would wait so late into the season to sweat me about that football gear. What was so ironic about it? Our next game was vs Washington high school. Go Go told me to go talk to Lehman and get back for practice as soon as possible. After scrambling to catch 2 city buses to Washington, I made my way to coach Lehman's office. As I walked into the room, I was confronted by the smugness and cockiness of the coach. Sitting at his desk with an imposing look on his face, he asked me, "was it worth it?" "Was transferring to Marshall really worth it?"

"They're not giving you the ball!" Lehman stated. "You didn't have to transfer. You overreacted, Perdue."

"You told me that I would never be more than a second-string fullback on your team." I reminded him. Lehman then stated that I gave up too easily. "Where is my gear at?" He quipped. I told him that I left everything in my locker. Lehman then points to a sack of football gear in a corner of the room and says, "does that look familiar?" Most of the items that were in the sack were assigned to me, when I tried to play at Washington high school. Apparently, some of my ex-teammates purged my locker after they realized I had quit the team. Lehman declared that the matter was settled, and he hoped that I had learned a valuable lesson. Then he thanked me for coming. I hustled out of the school, and to the bus stop so I could hurry back to Marshall for football practice.

On the rides back to practice, I tried to figure out why it was so important to coach Lehman to confront me about quitting his team. The encounter after the Riverside game was weird and humiliating, but the threat of having me suspended for the Marshall vs Washington game spoke of something else. "Why is this dude sweating me?" I thought. He didn't want to give me an opportunity, so why does he care where I complete my high school education? Was Lehman that vain and controlling of a coach? So vain, that he just had to take advantage of any opportunity he had to rub my nose in what he may have thought was a mistake? Was my transfer a blow to his ego? I don't know, but after much reflection on the matter years later, I've come to the conclusion that coach Lehman knew that I had the potential to be a good football player. I also think that Lehman may have realized that he too, had failed me with a lack of communication. Coach Lehman is a football legend in City conference football in Milwaukee. He built a strong football program at Washington high school. Coach Lehman won a lot of football games and developed a lot of college and pro caliber talent.

Although my experience with Lehman wasn't the greatest, I still have respect for the man.

After a motivated week of practice, it's now game time vs Washington. On our first offensive series, Go Go starts the game by giving me the first two plays. A fullback dive up the middle and a fullback trap. I moved the chains for a 1st down. Go Go took me out for a breather. I was geeked up! Usually, coach Go would start me but give Jerry the first carry or two. But Go Go knew that this game was special to me. I don't think that Go Go respected how Lehman threatened my eligibility to play. Although I was ready to run the rock down the Purgolders' throats, Coach had a different game plan. I only received 2 more carries the entire game. On defense, I made some tackles and had some QB pressures, but I really wanted to make more of an impact on offense. Coach Lehman got the last laugh, and the win.

At this point of the season, it's becoming obvious that our football team isn't going to make the state play-offs. Some guys are already checking out mentally, displaying minimum effort and a lack of focus in practice. And as the season was quickly coming to an end, I sensed that most of my teammates were becoming more relieved than regretful. The losing had taken its toll, and playing football just wasn't that fun anymore. The grind was almost over, and guys were looking forward to the next sport or activity. We finished our season with a win over Madison high school, (I would later be given my first coaching opportunity at Madison high school, years later.) and an overall record of 3-6.

It was my senior year, and my high school football career was over. My play wasn't outstanding enough to draw interest from college football recruiters and scouts, and I didn't know how to reach out to smaller programs that allowed walk-on opportunities. All I knew is that it was a long, hard journey to validate myself as a football player. Once again, I had lost my love for the game. I was now truly ready to hang up the cleats. I may not have reached my full potential on the football field, but the game itself gave me so much more. The game of football gave me the tools to develop self-discipline. The game of football taught me to honor commitments. And most importantly, the game of football helped me develop resilience in times of adversity.

After I graduated I remained bitter toward the sport of football for a long time. I didn't even have a desire to watch football on TV anymore. But the life lessons that I learned from football were always applied to every aspect of my life. Some kids are unselfish and wouldn't mind changing positions playing their favorite sports. For some, the opportunity to just be able to play is enough satisfaction. But some kids are born to play a certain sport, and certain positions that pertain to that sport. I was born and built to play football. And I was born and built to forever be a FULLBACK.

THE END

.

www.ingramcontent.com/pod-product-compliance
Lightning Source LLC
Chambersburg PA
CBHW061457250726
48657CB00005B/1653